Spain: Not like a tourist

Brittney Pilarcik

Spain: Not Like a Tourist is a loving roast of everything *not* to do when you land in Spain convinced you already understand it.

This book is not a guide to monuments, must-see sights, or the "best paella near you." It's a field manual for cultural survival — a catalog of assumptions, habits, and well-meaning mistakes that instantly mark you as *that* foreigner.

If you've ever wondered why locals sigh when you order sangria, why dinner starts when you're ready for bed, or why everyone disappears in August, this book is for you. Read it before you arrive, after you embarrass yourself, or while you're living in Spain and slowly realizing the problem might be you.

Consider this your unofficial introduction to Spain

1. Assume everyone speaks English and refuse to learn a single word of Spanish.

2. Pronounce "gracias" as "GRAY-SHUS" and "Barcelona" as "BAR-CEL-OWN-UH."

3. Correct a Spaniard's Spanish because you took Duolingo for a week.

4. Say "tacos" are your favorite Spanish food.

5. Assume "paella" is pronounced "pie-ella" and order it everywhere, even at breakfast.

6. Use Latin American Spanish slang and be shocked when people don't understand.

7. Confidently say "Adiós" every time you leave a shop instead of "Hasta luego."

8. Call Castilian Spanish "real Spanish" in front of a Catalan.

9. Order sangria in Madrid and wonder why the locals look disgusted.

10. Ask for ketchup on your seafood paella.

11. Be confused when your "Spanish omelette" doesn't come in a tortilla.

12. Show up at a restaurant at 5 PM, demand dinner, and complain about their "weird schedule."

13. Drink a cappuccino after 11 AM and ask why people are staring at you.

14. Order a "tapas sampler" at a restaurant with laminated menus.

15. Cut in line at a crowded tapas bar because "no one told me there was a system."

16. Eat a bocadillo with a fork and knife.

17. Look for breakfast options that aren't a croissant or a piece of toast with tomato.

18. Try to find a decent iced coffee.

19. Ask if they have tacos al pastor.

20. Greet people with a firm handshake instead of two kisses.

21. Assume all Spaniards take a three-hour siesta every day.

22. Call someone "Señorita" in a professional setting.

23. Expect customer service to be fast, friendly, or remotely helpful.

24. Wear shorts in winter and ask why people are staring at you.

25. Yell "olé!" at inappropriate times.

26. Be horrified when your coworker calls you "guapo/guapa" and think it's harassment.

27. Try to make small talk about politics five minutes into meeting someone.

28. Bring your own booze to a bar because "drinks are too expensive."

29. Expect people to form an orderly queue instead of aggressively crowding the entrance.

30. Go out for drinks at 9 PM and wonder why the bars are empty.

31. Order a beer instead of a gin & tonic at a fancy cocktail bar.

32. Show up to a nightclub at midnight and complain it's empty.

33. Leave a club at 3 AM and think you "stayed out late."

34. Expect a cocktail to be more than just pure alcohol and a single ice cube.

35. Refuse to dance because you're embarrassed, even though everyone else is drunk.

36. Ask why there are ham legs hanging from the ceiling.

37. Order a mojito at a traditional Spanish bar.

38. Expect bars to have free WiFi or care about your credit card.

39. Go to Ibiza and think you're going to "relax."

40. Take a taxi from the airport when there's a perfectly good metro.

41. Try to rent a car and be shocked when it's manual transmission.

42. Expect a bus to arrive on time.

43. Ask why the high-speed train (AVE) isn't cheaper.

44. Rent a bike in Seville in the middle of August.

45. Refuse to take a siesta, thinking "I'll power through."

46. Try to find a Starbucks in a small town.

47. Get stuck in a Sunday ghost town, wondering why nothing is open.

48. Expect the metro to have air conditioning in summer.

49. Assume the beach vendors selling mojitos actually have licenses.

50. Go to the beach at noon and wonder why you're the only person there.

51. Think sunscreen is for weaklings.

52. Wear flip-flops everywhere, including restaurants.

53. Try to use a beach towel the size of a napkin.

54. Be horrified when someone near you sunbathes topless.

55. Refuse to buy a €1 beer from the beach vendor and then complain about being thirsty.

56. Expect to get your personal space at a crowded beach in Málaga.

57. Insist on swimming right next to the buoys because "I'm a strong swimmer."

58. Go to San Sebastián and expect warm beach water.

59. Be the only person actually swimming while everyone else just wades

60. Declare Gaudí's work "unfinished" and offer to help complete it

61. Stand in front of Guernica asking "But why didn't Picasso use more colors?"

62. Mistake La Sagrada Familia for a Halloween decoration gone wrong

63. Loudly proclaim "This is just like Las Vegas!" at the Alhambra

64. Try to convince the security guard at the Prado that your Instagram following qualifies you as a "professional photographer"

65. Attempt to correct a tour guide about the age of Roman ruins because "I read a blog"

66. Schedule meetings at 2pm, then wonder why everyone's at lunch

67. Send urgent emails on August 15th and expect immediate responses

68. Insist on "casual Friday" at a workplace where people wear suits to the beach

69. Try to network at a business lunch by refusing to drink wine

70. Start a PowerPoint presentation without first discussing family, football, and food for 45 minutes

71. Tell a Basque person "Oh, that's in Spain, right?"

72. Confidently explain to Catalans that Barcelona is "basically Madrid's sister city"

73. Ask someone from Galicia why they don't speak "proper Spanish"

74. Tell someone from the Canary Islands "but you're basically African"

75. Attempt to order patatas bravas in Valencia while refusing to try paella

76. Demand a "proof of payment" receipt for your €1.20 coffee

77. Expect your landlord to fix anything within the first three months

78. Try to pay with a €500 note at a corner shop

79. Ask why there's no air conditioning in your 300-year-old apartment

80. Complain about the lack of dryers in a country with 300 days of sunshine

81. Show up to La Tomatina in your best white designer clothes

82. Attempt to "run with the bulls" while live-streaming

83. Wear flip-flops to San Fermín and wonder why your feet hurt

84. Ask when the "evening portion" of Feria de Abril starts

85. Complain that Las Fallas is "too noisy" and "starts too late"

86. Attempt to explain Spanish wine regions to a bodega owner because you "took a course once"

87. Insist on splitting the bill exactly by item at a group dinner

88. Try to organize a "quick working lunch" at 1pm

89. Show up to a Spanish wedding in black and wonder why people look concerned

90. Leave a dinner party at midnight because "it's getting late"

91. Correct a Spanish Literature professor about Don Quixote because "you saw the movie"

92. Tell everyone you're "basically a local" after your 2-week study abroad in Salamanca

93. Write your thesis on "Spanish Culture" based entirely on Hemingway's observations

94. Insist on teaching your Spanish professor about the "proper use" of vosotros

95. Declare yourself an expert on García Lorca after reading one poem on Pinterest

96. Ask if the Mezquita in Córdoba is "some kind of fancy mosque"

97. Wonder why everything closes during Semana Santa - "isn't it just Easter?"

98. Try to high-five a priest during a processional

99. Ask if the Reconquista was "some kind of Spanish fiesta"

100. Complain that Santiago de Compostela's pilgrimage route "needs more Ubers"

101. Wear a Real Madrid jersey to a Barcelona bar

102. Ask why they don't play "real football" during a La Liga match

103. Suggest that padel is "just lazy tennis"

104. Wonder why everyone stops talking when El Clásico starts

105. Try to explain American football to locals during the Champions League final

106. Wear socks with sandals to the beach club in Marbella

107. Sport a flamenco dress to a regular dinner because "it's authentic"

108. Refuse to remove your baseball cap in church because "it's designer"

109. Wear a "Kiss Me I'm Spanish" t-shirt to a business meeting

110. Show up to a winter wedding in summer linen because "it's Spain"

111. Try to pay with Turkish Lira because "it's all Europe"

112. Expect stores to accept your American Express

113. Ask why shops don't price everything in Bitcoin

114. Demand a discount because "the economy is bad"

115. Refuse to carry cash because "everywhere must take Apple Pay"

116. Demand to see a doctor at 3 PM during siesta

117. Insist your travel insurance covers bullfighting injuries

118. Ask for "gluten-free paella" at a traditional restaurant

119. Expect a pharmacy to sell you antibiotics without a prescription

120. Complain about the "weird-tasting" tap water in Madrid

121. Ask why they don't use more air conditioning in a drought

122. Complain about olive trees "making a mess" in Jaén

123. Suggest they "just add more sand" to eroding beaches

124. Wonder why everyone uses "tiny cars" instead of SUVs

125. Try to recycle your sangria pitcher at a bar

126. Ask if Almodóvar is "some kind of dance"

127. Suggest that flamenco needs "more modern beats"

128. Wonder why Spanish TV shows don't have laugh tracks

129. Try to explain Netflix to your 90-year-old Spanish host family

130. Ask why Spanish radio plays "so much Spanish music"

131. Expect central heating in Andalusia

132. Complain about the lack of carpeting in a Mediterranean apartment

133. Ask for the elevator in a 16th-century building

134. Wonder why your balcony doesn't have American-style screens

135. Demand a "quiet room" in the center of Madrid during Las Fiestas

136. Try to register your emotional support pangolin

137. Ask why there are so many cats in the Roman ruins

138. Expect dogs to be banned from restaurants

139. Wonder why pigeons have "right of way" in historic plazas

140. Try to pet the guard dogs at the olive farms

141. Ask if El Greco was "sponsored by Pantone" due to his color choices

142. Try to "restore" another Jesus fresco because "that lady in Borja did it"

143. Suggest the Torres Kio needed "better feng shui"

144. Ask if Dalí's house in Cadaqués was "designed while drunk"

145. Wonder why they didn't "finish" the Roman aqueduct in Segovia

146. Order a "Spanish Coffee" at 4 AM in a club

147. Ask for a "quiet corner" at La Latina during a Madrid weekend

148. Try to close your tab every round because "that's normal"

149. Suggest starting the bachelor party at 6 PM

150. Ask for ice in your kalimotxo and watch the bartender's soul leave their body

151. Schedule a conference call during la sobremesa

152. Ask why nobody checks their email in August

153. Suggest "casual Thursdays" to complement "formal Fridays"

154. Try to leave work before your boss

155. Bring donuts to a morning meeting instead of jamón

156. Ask if there's a "fast pass" for the Camino de Santiago

157. Try to hail a taxi by whistling in Barcelona

158. Expect the last metro to run past 2 AM

159. Ask why trains don't run during a siesta

160. Complain about walking 500 meters in Cáceres' old town

161. Request "birthday sauce" instead of salsa rosa

162. Ask if the octopus in Galicia is "farm-raised"

163. Try to order gambas al ajillo "without the garlic"

164. Suggest improving gazpacho by heating it up

165. Ask for chorizo in your Valencia paella (the ultimate sin)

166. Wear a parka in Seville in September

167. Ask why they don't "just add more shade" in Córdoba in July

168. Complain about rain in Santiago de Compostela

169. Wonder why everyone's wearing coats when it's "only" 15°C

170. Expect snow in Granada in summer because "there are mountains"

171. Try to go shopping on a Sunday in Burgos

172. Ask for a "to-go" bag at El Corte Inglés café

173. Expect sales in August when everything's closed

174. Try to bargain at Zara

175. Ask for "regular" size instead of European numbers

176. Schedule student meetings during botellón time

177. Ask why there's no campus quad for frisbee

178. Expect university buildings to be "all in one place"

179. Try to form a study group during siesta

180. Ask where to buy a university hoodie

181. Bring a cooler the size of a small car to La Concha

182. Ask for a beach umbrella in Gijón in January

183. Try to reserve a spot on Barceloneta beach

184. Wear water shoes in Cádiz and call yourself "prepared"

185. Ask if the Mediterranean is "the same as the ocean"

186. Wear heels to run with the bulls

187. Ask when the "quiet time" starts during Las Fallas

188. Try to get a hotel in Pamplona for San Fermín "last minute"

189. Expect to maintain personal space at La Mercè

190. Ask if there's a "practice round" for La Tomatina

191. Say Manchester has better ham than Extremadura

192. Tell someone from Jerez that French champagne is better

193. Suggest that Italian olive oil is superior in Jaén

194. Ask why Bilbao doesn't "just copy" San Sebastián's food scene

195. Wonder why Valencia can't "share" their oranges with Madrid

196. Ask for the WiFi password at a 12th-century monastery

197. Try to use Google Maps in the ancient Jewish quarters

198. Expect 5G in the middle of the Picos de Europa

199. Ask why your phone doesn't work in the Caves of Altamira

200. Look for a podcast about "authentic Spanish culture" made by expats

201. Ask where to find "Spanish" food in San Sebastián

202. Try to understand Euskera by using Google Translate

203. Call a pintxos bar a "tapas bar" in Bilbao

204. Ask if txakoli is "just unfinished champagne"

205. Wonder why people get offended when you say "gracias" instead of "eskerrik asko"

206. Assume the sardana is "just a slow flamenco"

207. Ask why they "copied" Spanish during a calçotada

208. Try to order sangria at a vermutería

209. Wear red and yellow in Barcelona during a referendum

210. Ask why they need their "own language" when Spanish exists

211. Complain about the rain in Vigo "ruining your vacation"

212. Ask if they serve "regular octopus" instead of pulpo á feira

213. Wonder why Santiago de Compostela isn't "more modern"

214. Try to order fish inland because "all of Galicia is coastal"

215. Ask if Galician is "just Portuguese with a lisp"

216. Expect to find flamenco shows in every Sevilla restaurant

217. Ask why they "talk so fast" in Córdoba

218. Try to order "Alhambra beer" in Sevilla

219. Wear high heels on Ronda's cobblestone streets

220. Ask for ketchup with your pescaíto frito in Málaga

221. Tell locals you prefer Barcelona's lifestyle

222. Try to find parking near Gran Vía "just for a minute"

223. Ask why Andalucian's don't have their own language

224. Expect peace and quiet in La Latina on a Sunday

225. Wonder why everyone's eating dinner at midnight in Malasaña

226. Again, try to ask for chorizo in your paella (cardinal sin)!

227. Wear your fallas outfit to a regular dinner

228. Expect beaches to be empty during Las Fallas

229. Ask why they "copied" Catalan

230. Try to eat horchata with a spoon

231. Ask if you can day-trip from Mallorca to Tenerife

232. Expect Ibiza to be peaceful in August

233. Ask why Canarian Spanish "sounds different"

234. Try to find authentic paella in Lanzarote

235. Wonder why Menorca isn't "more like Mallorca"

236. Wear beachwear in Asturias in July

237. Ask why they don't serve gazpacho in Santander

238. Expect warm water beaches in A Coruña

239. Try to find bullfighting in Gijón

240. Wonder why sidra doesn't come in bottles with labels

241. Ask if the Moors left Spain "voluntarily"

242. Suggest the Romans "didn't leave much behind"

243. Wonder if Franco was "just misunderstood"

244. Ask if Columbus was "basically Spanish"

245. Try to explain Spanish history to a local based on "Game of Thrones"

246. Take selfies with nazarenos during Semana Santa

247. Ask why there's "another church" in every plaza

248. Wear shorts to enter the Mezquita

249. Expect cathedrals to close for siesta

250. Wonder why everything's closed on Sunday

251. Expect meetings to start on time in August

252. Try to schedule anything important for Friday afternoon

253. Ask why three-hour lunches aren't "inefficient"

254. Expect quick decisions without committee consensus

255. Wonder why nobody responds to emails during fiestas

256. Use "tu" with your professor

257. Say "de nada" in Catalunya expecting gratitude

258. Use Mexican slang in Salamanca

259. Ask why they don't pronounce their "h"s

260. Try to use vosotros in Latin America

261. Assume all Spaniards love bullfighting

262. Expect everyone to know flamenco

263. Think all Spanish women wear flamenco dresses

264. Ask why they're "so obsessed" with jamón

265. Wonder why coffee isn't served in paper cups

266. Ask where the nearest Starbucks is in a pueblo

267. Expect English menus in village restaurants

268. Try to find an open shop during siesta in a small town

269. Ask why they don't have more "tourist activities"

270. Wonder why the whole town knows you're there

271. Ask why stores don't open 24/7

272. Expect fast food to be popular in small towns

273. Wonder why everyone doesn't speak English

274. Try to find a dryer in your apartment

275. Ask why they don't have "normal" breakfast

276. Ask if they can "modernize" the historic center

277. Wonder why buildings don't have A/C units

279. Ask why streets aren't "straighter"

280. Try to find parking in a medieval town center

281. Ask for "Spanish tacos"

282. Expect dinner before 9 PM

283. Ask why coffee isn't "grande" sized

284. Wonder why seafood isn't "cooked through"

285. Try to find pineapple on pizza

286. Ask for "regular" paella in San Sebastián

287. Expect ice in your drinks

288. Wonder why bread isn't free

289. Try to find "mild" chorizo

290. Ask for "authentic Mexican food"

291. Wonder why tortilla doesn't come in a wrap

292. Expect free refills

293. Ask for decaf after dinner

294. Try to find "light" versions of traditional dishes

295. Wonder why there's no ranch dressing

296. Ask for "quick service" during lunch rush

297. Expect vegetarian options in a traditional mesón

298. Try to find ketchup for your patatas bravas

299. Ask why wine is cheaper than water

300. Wonder why nobody drinks light beer

301. Ask if Picasso "couldn't afford more colors" during his Blue Period

302. Try to find the "Instagram filter" Velázquez used in Las Meninas

303. Wonder if El Bosco was "on something" while painting

304. Ask if Dalí's melting clocks "need new batteries"

305. Suggest Miró "let his kid draw that one"

306. Ask if Don Quixote is "based on a true story"

307. Wonder why García Lorca didn't "write something happier"

308. Try to find the "SparkNotes version" of Cervantes

309. Ask if Carmen is "that girl from the opera"

310. Suggest that Machado "needed to get out more"

311. Call a zambomba "a broken drum" in Jerez

312. Ask where the castanets are during a Basque folk concert

313. Try to dance sevillanas at a sardana circle

314. Wonder why there's "no DJ" at a jota performance

315. Request "Despacito" from a flamenco guitarist

316. Ask if Almodóvar makes "those Mexican soap operas"

317. Wonder why Penélope Cruz "doesn't sound Spanish" in Hollywood

318. Try to find the beach from "Vicky Cristina Barcelona" in Madrid

319. Ask if Antonio Banderas learned Spanish "after Zorro"

320. Expect all Spanish films to have flamenco soundtracks

321. Wear a Mexican sombrero to a Spanish wedding

322. Sport a "flamenco-inspired" outfit to a business meeting

323. Ask why nobody wears matador outfits casually

324. Try to find flip-flops appropriate for Paseo del Prado

325. Wonder why your "Spanish look" Pinterest board isn't working

326. Ask if the University of Salamanca is "like Harvard but Spanish"

327. Try to form a fraternity at Complutense

328. Expect campus housing in central Madrid

329. Wonder why there's no "Spanish Ivy League"

330. Ask for extra credit in a Spanish university

331. Ask when Real Madrid plays Barcelona "in the World Cup"

332. Wonder why there's no commercial breaks during La Liga

333. Try to start the wave during a crucial penalty kick

334. Expect cheerleaders at a football match

335. Ask which team Messi plays for in Madrid

336. Ask if the Royal Palace has a "Disney influence"

337. Wonder if Queen Letizia "knows Kate Middleton"

338. Try to find the Spanish crown jewels "like in London"

339. Ask if the king takes the metro

340. Expect to see royalty shopping at El Corte Inglés

341. Try to use PayPal at a 200-year-old tavern

342. Ask why your phone doesn't translate Euskera properly

343. Wonder why there's no Uber in your medieval village

344. Expect 5G in the Picos de Europa

345. Try to find a charging station in the Alhambra

346. Ask why the Mediterranean "isn't as blue as the Caribbean"

347. Try to surf in Valencia in August

348. Wonder why Galician beaches aren't "more tropical"

349. Expect warm water in the Cantabrian Sea

350. Ask if you can see Africa from Málaga beach

351. Ask if they can "add an elevator" to the Giralda

352. Wonder why Toledo isn't "more modernized"

353. Try to find the "authentic" part of Benidorm

354. Ask why they don't "update" the Roman walls

355. Suggest solar panels for the Sagrada Familia

356. Ask why they can't "just get along" in Catalunya

357. Wonder why there are "so many" political parties

358. Try to explain American bipartisanism in a Spanish bar

359. Expect everyone to agree on Franco's legacy

360. Ask why they need autonomous communities

361. Try to schedule a meeting during fútbol finals

362. Ask why stores close for "random saints"

363. Expect quick service during puente season

364. Wonder why nobody works in August

365. Try to find office space with "open floor plans"

366. Ask why they don't have "drive-through pharmacies"

367. Wonder why doctors don't work during siesta

368. Try to find "Spanish NyQuil"

369. Expect 24/7 grocery stores with pharmacies

370. Ask why they don't have "more commercials for medicine"

371. Try to find a school cafeteria serving pizza

372. Ask why students go home for lunch

373. Wonder why there's no "Spanish SAT"

374. Expect parent-teacher meetings during siesta

375. Try to understand why September is "still summer"

376. Ask why they don't "just add more beaches" in Barcelona

377. Wonder why solar panels aren't "everywhere" in Asturias

378. Try to find recycling bins for "every type of plastic"

379. Expect green lawns in Almería

380. Ask why they don't have more palm trees in Galicia

381. Try to organize a "quick" Spanish wedding

382. Ask why the ceremony isn't in English too

383. Wonder why there's no "cash bar" option

384. Expect the party to end at midnight

385. Try to find a wedding registry at El Corte Inglés

386. Ask why high-speed trains don't stop in every village

387. Wonder why nobody uses "normal" yellow taxis

388. Try to find parking in central Cádiz

389. Expect buses to run on time during fiestas

390. Ask why everyone doesn't just drive everywhere

391. Try to find a quiet spot during La Tamborrada

392. Ask why nobody celebrates Thanksgiving

393. Wonder why Christmas lasts until January 6

394. Expect Halloween to be "like in America"

395. Try to find Black Friday deals in February

396. Ask why Three Kings Day isn't "more efficient"

397. Wonder why nobody does baby showers

398. Try to organize a gender reveal party

399. Expect bachelor parties to be "one night only"

400. Ask why weddings don't have "open mic" speeches

401. Ask where the "tourist attractions" are in Mérida's Roman ruins

402. Try to find "mild" pimentón in La Vera

403. Wonder why everyone's obsessed with jamón ibérico in Montánchez

404. Expect air conditioning in July in Trujillo

405. Ask if the storks are "part of a zoo exhibit"

406. Try to find beachfront property in Burgos

407. Ask why Valladolid isn't "more like Madrid"

408. Wonder why Segovia's aqueduct "needs all those arches"

409. Expect late-night dining options in Soria

410. Try to find English menus in Palencia

411. Ask if the Pyrenees are "walkable in an afternoon"

412. Wonder why Zaragoza isn't "more famous"

413. Try to find beach volleyball courts in Teruel

414. Expect mild winters in Huesca

415. Ask why they don't "modernize" the mudéjar architecture

Ask for "just any wine" in Haro

Try to pronounce Tempranillo as "tempo-nillo"

Wonder why they don't make white Rioja "more popular"

Expect wine tours to start at 9 AM

Ask if they have "wine slushies" at a bodega

Ask why they grow lemons "when they have oranges"

Wonder if the Mar Menor is "just a big pool"

Try to find "regular" paparajotes without lemon leaves

424. Expect vegetables to be "optional" in Murcian cuisine

425. Ask why they need "so many types of peppers"

426. Wear white to Las Fallas thinking it's "like La Tomatina"

427. Ask when the bulls show up at the Cascamorras

428. Try to join the Tamborrada without knowing how to drum

429. Expect to stay clean during the Haro Wine Battle

430. Wonder why everyone's jumping over bonfires in Alicante

431. Ask for a "quick taxi" in a mountain village

432. Try to find durum wheat pasta in a traditional pueblo

433. Expect 24/7 pharmacies in La Alpujarra

434. Ask why village dogs "don't use leashes"

435. Wonder why siesta is "still a thing" in small towns

436. Wear a raincoat in Almería in August

437. Expect snow in Málaga because "it has mountains"

438. Try to plan outdoor activities in Galicia without a backup plan

439. Ask why Santiago has "so much unnecessary rain"

440. Wonder why nobody's at the beach at noon in July

441. Try to schedule a "working lunch" during sobremesa

442. Ask why they don't have "drive-through everything"

443. Expect same-day delivery in a medieval town

444. Wonder why shops close for "random saints"

445. Try to find a "quick breakfast place" at 7 AM

446. Ask for fish paella in Madrid

447. Try to find patatas bravas in a high-end Basque restaurant

448. Expect gazpacho to be served hot in Barcelona

449. Wonder why there's no "fusion tapas" in traditional Sevilla bars

450. Ask for "mild" mojo picón in the Canary Islands

451. Use "vale" in Barcelona expecting no reactions

452. Try to speak Mexican Spanish in Valladolid

453. Ask why they need "so many words for bread"

454. Expect everyone in Valencia to be bilingual

455. Wonder why Galician "sounds like Portuguese"

456. Expect tropical waters in Asturias

457. Try to surf in the Mediterranean

458. Ask why Cantabrian beaches aren't "more like Benidorm"

459. Wear a wetsuit in Cádiz in August

460. Wonder why La Concha isn't "more crowded" in January

461. Ask if the Moors "visited often" during the Reconquista

462. Try to find Columbus's "first stop" in Madrid

463. Wonder why they don't "update" cave paintings

464. Expect the Spanish Inquisition to be "just a Monty Python joke"

465. Ask if El Cid "has a Twitter account"

466. Try to high-five Jesus floats during Semana Santa

467. Ask why they need "so many virgin statues"

468. Expect churches to be "more modern" in Barcelona

469. Wonder why processions "take so long"

470. Try to find "express mass" during important festivals

471. Try to charge your phone in a 12th-century tapas bar

472. Ask for the WiFi password at a Roman bath

473. Attempt to Uber through the narrow streets of Toledo

474. Tag yourself at "The Real Atlantis" in a Galician storm

475. Try to livestream your first bull encounter

476. Attempt to recreate "Salt Bae" with jamón carving

477. Strike a "holding up" pose with the Sagrada Familia

478. Try to get a "quiet photo" at La Rambla

479. Expect to be alone at Park Güell's famous bench

480. Ask someone to take your photo during the bull run

481. Hold up the line taking paella photos "for the gram"

482. Try to rearrange a traditional tapas spread for "better composition"

483. Ask the chef to "make it look prettier" at a 100-year-old tavern

484. Demand "better lighting" for your churros at 4 AM

485. Stage a wine-pouring photo with a €300 Rioja

486. Start pregaming at 7 PM for a club that opens at 2 AM

487. Try to order a Long Island Iced Tea at a vermutería

488. Ask for the bouncer's Instagram at Kapital

489. Expect to find "quiet corners" at Ushuaïa Ibiza

490. Wonder why everyone's just starting dinner at midnight

491. Try to split the bill on a first date

492. Show up "on time" for a Spanish dinner date

493. Suggest Netflix and chill instead of a paseo

494. Expect to meet the parents after three dates

495. Try to leave the date before 2 AM

496. Schedule a "quick meeting" during tortilla time

497. Try to eat lunch at your desk

498. Ask why nobody answers emails on a puente

499. Expect productivity during fútbol matches

500. Wonder why your colleagues think 35 vacation days "isn't enough"

501. Try to validate your metro ticket while being pushed by 50 people

502. Ask why the bus driver is taking a cigarette break mid-route

503. Expect personal space on the last metro

504. Wonder why everyone runs for the train that "comes every 5 minutes"

505. Try to find the "express line" to the airport during a strike

506. Ask for "just antibiotics" at the pharmacy

507. Expect the doctor to rush your consultation

508. Try to find urgent care during siesta

509. Wonder why your prescription looks like "ancient hieroglyphics"

510. Ask if there's a "faster way" to get universal healthcare

511. Try to "dodge" tomatoes at La Tomatina

512. Ask for a "less noisy spot" during Las Fallas

513. Wear designer clothes to a wine fight

514. Expect to find your friends in the Carnival crowd

515. Try to stay clean during a color powder festival

516. Leave a Sunday lunch before the third dessert

517. Try to help in abuela's kitchen without permission

518. Ask for the "quick version" of family gossip

519. Expect to eat dinner before 10 PM

520. Wonder why the volume increases with each course

521. Wear a Real Madrid scarf in the Camp Nou gift shop

522. Ask why everyone's crying over a 0-0 draw

523. Try to explain American football during El Clásico

524. Suggest they "add cheerleaders" to La Liga

525. Wonder why bar TVs don't show "other sports" during fútbol

526. Expect stores to open "just for a minute" during siesta

527. Try to return something without a 17-page form

528. Ask for a "to-go bag" at El Corte Inglés

529. Wonder why the sales clerk isn't "more cheerful"

530. Try to shop on a Sunday in a non-tourist area

531. Wear a raincoat in Sevilla in August

532. Ask why nobody else is sweating

533. Expect air conditioning everywhere

534. Try to find indoor activities in "sunny Spain"

535. Wonder why people are wearing coats in 20°C weather

536. Tell a Basque their pintxos are "just like tapas"

537. Ask a Catalan why they "copied Spanish"

538. Tell a Galician their octopus is "basically calamari"

539. Suggest that paella is "better in Madrid"

540. Wonder why regions "need their own languages"

541. Try to find a "quiet bar" at 3 AM

542. Ask why children are still awake

543. Expect restaurants to have "early bird specials"

544. Wonder why breakfast places open "so late"

545. Try to order a decaf after dinner

546. Ask for the bar's TikTok handle

547. Try to find a "phone-free zone" in Plaza Mayor

548. Expect everyone to use contactless payment

549. Wonder why there's no app for siesta timing

550. Ask if the churros are "gluten-free"

551. Ask for the "authentic experience" on Las Ramblas

552. Try to find the "real flamenco" in a tourist show

553. Expect reasonable prices near major attractions

554. Wonder why locals don't eat at "tourist menus"

555. Ask if the sangria is "craft-made"

556. Try to form a queue at a crowded bar

557. Expect personal space in the metro

558. Ask why everyone's "so close" while walking

559. Wonder why people are shouting their conversations

560. Try to find a "quiet corner" in a plaza during summer

561. Ask your Spanish grandma to "just send a quick text"

562. Try to explain TikTok to your tía who still uses a Nokia

563. Show your abuelo how to use Instagram for his jamón photos

564. Expect your elderly neighbor to accept digital payments

565. Ask the village elder to "check their email" about the festival

566. Try to eat dinner while scrolling Instagram

567. Ask abuela if her cocido recipe is "on Pinterest"

568. Suggest DoorDash to your traditional Spanish mother

569. Wonder why grandpa insists on three-hour lunches

570. Try to convince your parents that brunch is "better than sobremesa"

571. Send your grandmother an emoji-only response

572. Expect your great-aunt to understand "LOL"

573. Try to make a family WhatsApp group with the village elders

574. Ask your grandfather to "just FaceTime" instead of visiting

575. Suggest a Zoom call for Sunday family lunch

576. Ask why the plastic-covered sofa "isn't aesthetic"

577. Suggest minimalism to your trinket-collecting abuela

578. Try to explain why you don't want to display every family photo

579. Question why they keep empty olive oil bottles

580. Wonder why they won't throw away 30-year-old furniture

581. Wear ripped jeans to visit your grandmother

582. Try to explain streetwear to your traditional father

583. Ask why you need to "dress up" for a regular Sunday lunch

584. Suggest casual wear for church to your mother

585. Wonder why flip-flops aren't "appropriate" for dinner

586. Try to explain Netflix to your radio-loving grandfather

587. Ask your grandmother why she needs so many telenovelas

588. Suggest video games instead of dominoes

589. Wonder why they still buy physical newspapers

590. Try to introduce podcasts to your news-at-9 parents

591. Explain remote work to your "office-only" uncle

592. Try to convince abuela that freelancing is "a real job"

593. Justify your startup idea to your government-employee parents

594. Ask why you need to "dress formally" for a phone interview

595. Wonder why they don't understand "digital nomad" lifestyle

596. Suggest vegan options for traditional family recipes

597. Try to explain keto to your bread-loving grandmother

598. Ask for gluten-free alternatives at a family gathering

599. Propose smoothie bowls instead of traditional breakfast

600. Wonder why they don't understand intermittent fasting

601. Try to explain dating apps to your traditional aunt

602. Tell your grandparents you met your partner online

603. Explain why you don't want to marry at 25

604. Ask why you need to invite the whole village to your wedding

605. Justify living with roommates past 30

606. Explain CrossFit to your walk-around-the-plaza grandmother

607. Try to convince abuela that not all illness require tea

608. Suggest meditation apps to your worry-bead wielding grandfather

609. Ask why every ailment needs Vicks VapoRub

610. Wonder why they don't trust "modern medicine"

611. Try to explain cryptocurrency to your peseta-missing grandfather

612. Suggest online banking to your cash-only grandmother

613. Explain why you don't want to buy property right away

614. Ask why they keep money "under the mattress"

615. Wonder why they don't trust digital payments

616. Try to teach your grandfather to use a smartphone

617. Explain why you need more than one device

618. Ask your grandmother to stop printing her emails

619. Wonder why they write down TV schedules

620. Try to explain cloud storage to your floppy-disk-saving uncle

621. Suggest IKEA furniture to your antique-loving family

622. Try to explain why you don't need lace doilies

623. Ask why every room needs a religious image

624. Wonder why plastic flowers are "better than real ones"

625. Try to convince them that minimalism isn't "being poor"

626. Propose a "small" Christmas dinner for under 30 people

627. Try to skip the Three Kings parade

628. Suggest Secret Santa instead of giving everyone gifts

629. Ask why Easter needs a whole week of processions

630. Wonder why every saint needs a celebration

631. Explain why you prefer public transport

632. Try to convince them that walking is "actually nice"

633. Ask why every family member needs a car

634. Suggest carpooling to family events

635. Wonder why they won't try electric vehicles

636. Play reggaeton at a family gathering

637. Try to explain music streaming to your CD-collecting uncle

638. Ask why they need physical copies of everything

639. Suggest modern versions of traditional songs

640. Wonder why they don't understand your playlist

641. Try to explain recycling to your plastic-bag-saving grandmother

642. Suggest reducing meat consumption to your jamón-loving family

643. Ask why they need their car for a 5-minute walk

644. Propose eco-friendly alternatives to traditional products

645. Wonder why they keep all plastic containers

646. Try to explain why you're learning Korean instead of improving your Spanish

647. Ask why they don't use language apps

648. Suggest online courses instead of traditional academies

649. Wonder why they insist on dubbed movies

650. Try to explain internet slang to your traditional relatives

651. Try to explain Instagram filters to your "just take the photo" grandmother

652. Ask your grandfather why he shares every Facebook post

653. Explain why your abuela shouldn't write entire conversations in WhatsApp status

654. Wonder why your aunt tags you in every Spanish meme

655. Try to teach your uncle that not every message needs "..."

656. Explain skincare routines to your "just use soap" grandmother

657. Try to convince your mother that natural gray hair is trendy

658. Ask why you need to dress up to go to the supermarket

659. Wonder why your aunt insists on buying you "proper clothes"

660. Try to explain Korean beauty products to your Nivea-loyal relatives

661. Suggest removing plastic fruit from the display bowl

662. Try to explain why you don't want heavy curtains in every room

663. Ask why there needs to be a TV in every room

664. Wonder why the "good room" is never used

665. Try to remove the plastic sofa covers

666. Explain why you want to buy pre-cut jamón

667. Try to introduce meal prep to your "fresh food only" family

668. Ask why you need five different types of olive oil

669. Wonder why the kitchen needs 47 different pots

670. Try to suggest an air fryer to your traditional cook grandmother

671. Explain CrossFit to your "walking is enough" grandparents

672. Try to convince them that gym membership isn't "wasting money"

673. Ask why swimming in winter is "dangerous"

674. Wonder why yoga is considered "not real exercise"

675. Try to explain HIIT to your siesta-loving relatives

676. Explain why you're not married at 25

677. Try to convince them that online dating isn't dangerous

678. Ask why you need to date someone from "a good family"

679. Wonder why they need to know your date's entire family history

680. Try to explain why you're not ready for children

681. Explain being a content creator to your "get a real job" parents

682. Try to convince them that remote work isn't "being lazy"

683. Ask why government jobs are the only "proper careers"

684. Wonder why entrepreneurship is considered risky

685. Try to explain digital marketing to your newspaper-reading uncle

686. Suggest brunch instead of traditional lunch

687. Try to skip the weekly family gathering for once

688. Ask why Sunday shopping is "morally wrong"

689. Wonder why you can't just "relax at home"

690. Try to explain why you need "me time"

691. Suggest ordering Christmas dinner instead of cooking for three days

692. Try to skip the 6-hour family lunch

693. Ask why New Year's grapes can't be pre-peeled

694. Wonder why Three Kings Day needs so much preparation

695. Try to explain why you want to travel during holidays

696. Explain probiotics to your "just eat yogurt" grandmother

697. Try to convince them that air conditioning won't make you sick

698. Ask why every illness needs chicken soup

699. Wonder why they don't trust any doctor under 50

700. Try to explain mental health therapy to your "just be happy" family

701. Expect the village dog to be leashed like in the city

702. Try to explain to visitors why all Spanish cats seem to live on rooftops

703. Wonder why your Spanish neighbors' dog is "guarding" their terrace 24/7

704. Ask why every pueblo has exactly 47 free-roaming cats

705. Try to find an "indoor cat" in a traditional Spanish neighborhood

706. Attempt to walk your dog during siesta in Sevilla

707. Try to explain dog beaches to your inland Spanish relatives

708. Ask why Mallorca's cats all live at the port

709. Wonder why Madrid dogs wear more clothes than humans

710. Try to find pet-friendly housing in Barcelona's Gothic Quarter

711. Tell your Spanish landlord you have "just a small dog"

712. Try to convince the local bar owner your dog is "tranquilo"

713. Ask why the village cats have a designated feeding schedule

714. Wonder why everyone in the pueblo knows your dog's name

715. Try to explain pet insurance to your "it's just a street cat" neighbors

716. Expect dogs to be allowed in restaurants

717. Try to keep your dog from greeting everyone on a paseo

718. Ask why your Spanish neighbor's cat visits every house for food

719. Wonder why everyone feeds the street cats except the "official" caretaker

720. Try to find a dog park that isn't just the plaza

701. Tell your grandparents you're skipping the family beach town for Thailand

702. Try to explain hostels to your "hotels only" parents

703. Ask why you can't explore Spain "without visiting relatives"

704. Wonder why every trip needs to include a family meeting

705. Try to convince them that camping is "actually fun"

706. Explain BlaBlaCar to your "only use trusted drivers" family

707. Try to convince them that budget airlines are safe

708. Ask why you need to take the "expensive train" instead of the bus

709. Wonder why they insist on driving 8 hours instead of flying

710. Try to explain why you prefer public transport to having a car

711. Tell your family you're staying in an Airbnb instead of Hotel Meliá

712. Try to explain couch-surfing to your horrified relatives

713. Ask why you need to book "only 4-star hotels"

714. Wonder why they won't try rural tourism

715. Try to convince them that hostels aren't "just for poor students"

716. Explain why you're visiting Cuenca instead of Benidorm

717. Try to convince them that Mallorca has more than beach resorts

718. Ask why Torremolinos is considered "the best vacation"

719. Wonder why they won't explore the Picos de Europa

720. Try to suggest a hiking trip instead of a beach holiday

721. Show your spontaneous booking to your "plan-six-months-ahead" parents

722. Try to explain last-minute deals to your "must book in advance" uncle

723. Ask why you need to pack "for every possible weather"

724. Wonder why they need three suitcases for a weekend trip

725. Try to travel with just a carry-on baggage

726. Explain why you want to try local food instead of Spanish restaurants abroad

727. Try to convince them street food is safe

728. Ask why you need to pack jamón for a three-day trip

729. Wonder why they won't try "exotic" cuisines

730. Try to explain why you don't need to eat at Spanish restaurants in London

731. Tell them you're spending money on experiences instead of shopping

732. Try to explain why you chose a cheaper hotel to stay longer

733. Ask why you need to buy souvenirs for the entire extended family

734. Wonder why they won't use travel reward cards

735. Try to convince them that luxury travel isn't the only way

736. Explain why you're doing a cooking class instead of beach lounging

737. Try to convince them that museum visits aren't "wasting vacation time"

738. Ask why every trip needs to include shopping

739. Wonder why they won't try adventure activities

740. Try to suggest cultural tours instead of resort activities

741. Tell them you chose a destination because of Instagram

742. Try to explain why you're documenting the entire trip

743. Ask why they need to call family every day while traveling

744. Wonder why they won't share photos online

745. Try to convince them that travel blogging is "actually useful"

746. Explain digital nomad life to your confused relatives

747. Try to convince them that working remotely while traveling is possible

748. Ask why you need to "save travel for retirement"

749. Wonder why they won't use travel apps

750. Try to explain why you're joining a travel community

www.ingramcontent.com/pod-product-compliance
Lightning Source LLC
Chambersburg PA
CBHW070449130626
46553CB00006B/2330